Sonnets of Love & Friendship

Sonnets of Love & Friendship

PASSION ❧ TESTIMONY ❧ FAITH

REMEMBRANCE ❧ AMONG THE GODS ❧ LOVE UNDONE

SPIRITUAL LOVE ❧ FRIENDSHIP

selected by

Holly Pell McConnaughy

BARNES
&NOBLE
B O O K S
N E W Y O R K

Introduction and compilation copyright © 1993
by Barnes & Noble, Inc.

This edition published by Barnes & Noble, Inc.

1993 Barnes & Noble Books

ISBN 1-56619-046-0

Book design by Charles Ziga, Ziga Design

Printed and bound in the United States of America

M 9 8 7 6 5 4 3

Contents

Testimony

Faith

Remembrance

Among the Gods

Love Undone

Spiritual Love

Friendship

Introduction

Nuns fret not at their convent's narrow room;
And hermits are contented with their cells;
And students with their pensive citadels;
Maids at the wheel, the weaver at his loom,
Sit blithe and happy; bees that soar for bloom,
High as the highest Peak of Furness-fells,
Will murmur by the hour in foxglove bells:
In truth the prison, unto which we doom
Ourselves, no prison is: and hence for me,
In sundry moods, 'twas pastime to be bound
Within the Sonnet's scanty plot of ground;
Pleased if some Souls (for such there needs must be)
Who have felt the weight of too much liberty,
Should find brief solace there, as I have found.

❤ WILLIAM WORDSWORTH

Given the stringent dictates of the sonnet form—fourteen lines and a limited variety of rhyme schemes—the diversity of poets who have chosen to write in this style is rather astounding. From John Donne to William Shakespeare, and from John Keats to Elizabeth Barrett Browning—not to mention the ubiquitous Anonymous from Elizabethan times—the sonnet is a well-respected and oft' used poetic form. Whether rhapsodizing over a true love's features or bemoaning the cruelty of love, eulogizing on the merits of a friend or comparing earthly life to celestial divinity, countless poets have accepted the stylistic confinement of the sonnet and perceived them as a rewarding challenge.

Set within the parameters of love and friendship, the sonnets in this book reflect the variety of forms that the sonnet can assume and the diversity of subject matter that may be addressed within fourteen brief lines. For sonnets can move, amuse, muse, or simply charm their readers. As Robert Burns wrote:

Fourteen, a sonneteer thy praises sings,
What magic mysteries in that number lie!

❤ HOLLY PELL McCONNAUGHY

Passion

Now!

Out of your whole life give but a moment!
All of your life that has gone before,
All to come after it,— so you ignore,
So you make perfect the present,— condense,
In a rapture of rage, for perfection's endowment,
Thought and feeling and soul and sense—
Merged in a moment which gives me at last
You around me for once, you beneath me, above me—
Me— sure that despite of time future, time past,—
This tick of our life-time's one moment you love me!
How long such suspension may linger? Ah, Sweet—
The moment eternal—just that and no more—
When ecstasy's utmost we clutch at the core
While cheeks burn, arms open, eyes shut and lips meet!

❤ ROBERT BROWNING

To the Ladies who Saw Me Crowned

What is there in the universal Earth
  More lovely than a wreath from the bay tree?
  Haply a halo round the moon—a glee
Circling from three sweet pair of lips in mirth;
And haply you will say the dewy birth
  Of morning roses—ripplings tenderly
  Spread by the halcyon's breath upon the sea—
But these comparisons are nothing worth.
Then is there nothing in the world so fair?
  The silvery tears of April? Youth of May?
Or June that breathes out life for butterflies?
  No—none of these can from my favourite bear
Away the palm—yet shall it ever pay
  Due reverence to your most sovereign eyes.

❤ JOHN KEATS

Although We Do Not All the Good We Love

Although we do not all the good we love,
But still, in love, desire to do the same;
Nor leave the sins we hate, but hating move
Our soul and body's powers their powers to tame;
The good we do God takes as done aright,
That we desire to do he takes as done;
The sin we shun he will with grace requite,
And not impute the sin we seek to shun.
But good desires produce no worser deeds,
For God doth both together lightly give,
Because he knows a righteous man must needs
By faith, that works by love, forever live.
　　Then to do nought but only in desire
　　Is love that burns, but burns like painted fire.

❤ JOHN DAVIES OF HEREFORD

Her First Season

He gazed her over, from her eyebrows down
    Even to her feet: he gazed so with the good
    Undoubting faith of fools, much as who should
Accost God for a comrade. In the brown
Of all her curls he seemed to think the town
    Would make an acquisition; but her hood
Was not the newest fashion, and his brood
Of lady-friends might scarce approve her gown.
If I did smile, 'twas faintly; for my cheeks
    Burned, thinking she'd be shown up to be sold,
    And cried about, in the thick jostling run
Of the loud world, till all the weary weeks
    Should bring her back to herself and to the old
Familiar face of nature and the sun.

❤ WILLIAM MICHAEL ROSSETTI

To Pandora

Go you, O winds that blow from north to south,
  Convey my secret sighs unto my sweet;
Deliver them from mine unto her mouth,
And make my commendations till we meet.
But if perhaps her proud aspiring sp'rit
Will not accept nor yet receive the same,
The breast and bulwark of her bosom beat,
Knock at her heart, and tell from whence you came;
Importune her, nor cease nor shrink for shame;
Sport with her curls of amber-colored hair,
And when she sighs, immix yourselves with thame,
Give her her own, and thus beguile the fair.
   Blow winds, fly sighs, where as my heart doth hant,
   And secretly commend me to my sanct.

❤ ALEXANDER CRAIG

Like As a Huntsman After Weary Chace

Like as a huntsman after weary chace,
   Seeing the game from him escapt away,
   Sits down to rest him in some shady place,
   With panting hounds beguiled of their prey:
So after long pursuit and vain assay,
   When I all weary had the chace forsook,
   The gentle dear return'd the selfsame way,
   Thinking to quench her thirst at the next brook:
There she beholding me with milder look,
   Sought not to fly, but fearless still did bide:
   Till I in hand her yet half trembling took,
   And with her own goodwill her firmly tied.
Strange thing meseem'd to see a beast so wild,
   So goodly won with her own will beguil'd.

❤ EDMUND SPENSER

On Lydia Distracted

With hairs, which for the wind to play with, hung,
   With her torn garments, and with naked feet,
   Fair Lydia dancing went from street to street,
Singing with pleasant voice her foolish song.

On her she drew all eyes in every place,
   And them to pity by her pranks did move,
   Which turned with gazing longer into Love
By the rare beauty of her charming face.

In all her frenzies, and her mimicries,
While she did Nature's richest gifts despise,
   There active Love did subtly play his part.

Her antic postures made her look more gay,
Her ragged clothes her treasures did display,
   And with each motion she ensnared a heart.

❤ PHILIP AYRES

Being Your Slave,
What Should I Do But Tend

$\mathcal{B}$eing your slave, what should I do but tend
Upon the hours and times of your desire?
I have no precious time at all to spend,
Nor services to do, till you require.
Nor dare I chide the world-without-end hour,
Whilst I, my sovereign, watch the clock for you,
Nor think the bitterness of absence sour,
When you have bid your servant once adieu.
Nor dare I question with my jealous thought
Where you may be, or your affairs suppose,
But like a sad slave stay and think of nought
Save where you are how happy you make those.
    So true a fool is love that in your will
    (Though you do any thing) he thinks no ill.

❤ WILLIAM SHAKESPEARE

Mine Eye, Myne Eare,
My Will, My Witt, My Harte

Mine Eye, myne eare, my will, my witt, my harte,
Did see, did heare, did like, discerne, did love,
Her face, her speche, her fashion, judgement, arte,
Which did charme, please, delighte, confounde and move.
Then fancie, humor, love, conceipte, and thoughte
Did soe drawe, force, intyse, perswade, devise,
That she was wonne, mov'd, caryed, compast, wrought,
To thinck me kinde, true, comelie, valyant, wise.
That heaven, earth, hell, my folly and her pride
Did worke, contrive, labor, conspire and sweare
To make me scorn'd, vile, cast of, bace, defyed
With her my love, my lighte, my life, my deare;
So that my harte, my witt, will, eare, and eye
Doth grieve, lament, sorrowe, dispaire and dye.

❤ ANONYMOUS

My Ladie's Presence
Makes the Roses Red

My Ladie's presence makes the Roses red,
   because to see her lips, they blush for shame:
   the Lillie's leaves (for envie) pale became,
   and her white hands in them this envie bred.
The Marigold the leaves abroad doth spred,
   because the sunne's; and her power is the same:
   the Violet of purple colour came,
   di'd in the bloud she made my hart to shed.
In briefe, all flowers from her theire vertue take;
   from her sweete breath theire sweete smells doo proceed;
   the living heate which her eie beames doth make,
   warmeth the ground, and quickeneth the seed:
      The raine wherewith she watereth these flowers
      falls from mine eyes, which she dissolves in showers.

❤ ANONYMOUS

Grief, Thou Hast Lost an Ever Ready Friend

Grief, thou hast lost an ever ready friend
  Now that the cottage Spinning-wheel is mute;
And Care—a comforter that best could suit
Her froward mood, and softliest reprehend;
And Love—a charmer's voice, that used to lend,
More efficaciously than aught that flows
From harp or lute, kind influence to compose
The throbbing pulse—else troubled without end:
Even Joy could tell, Joy craving truce and rest
From her own overflow, what power sedate
On those revolving motions did await
Assiduously—to soothe her aching breast;
And, to a point of just relief, abate
The mantling triumphs of a day too blest.

❤ WILLIAM WORDSWORTH

Since Brass, Nor Stone, Nor Earth, Nor Boundless Sea

Since brass, nor stone, nor earth, nor boundless sea,
But sad mortality o'ersways their power,
How with this rage shall beauty hold a plea,
Whose action is no stronger than a flower?
O how shall summer's honey breath hold out
Against the wrackful siege of batt'ring days,
When rocks impregnable are not so stout,
No gates of steel so strong, but Time decays?
O fearful meditation! where, alack,
Shall Time's best jewel from Time's chest lie hid?
Or what strong hand can hold his swift foot back?
Or who his spoil [of] beauty can forbid?
    O none, unless this miracle have might,
    That in black ink my love may still shine bright.

❤ WILLIAM SHAKESPEARE

Bright Star, would I were stedfast

Bright star, would I were stedfast as thou art—
Not in lone splendor hung aloft the night,
And watching, with eternal lids apart,
Like Nature's patient sleepless Eremite,
The moving waters at their priestlike task
Of pure ablution round earth's human shores,
Or gazing on the new soft fallen mask
Of snow upon the mountains and the moors:
No—yet still stedfast, still unchangeable,
Pillowed upon my fair love's ripening breast
To feel for ever its soft fall and swell,
Awake for ever in a sweet unrest;
Still, still to hear her tender-taken breath,
And so live ever—or else swoon to death.

❤ JOHN KEATS

Shall I Compare Thee to a Summer's Day?

Shall I compare thee to a summer's day?
Thou are more lovely and more temperate.
Rough winds do shake the darling buds of May,
And summer's lease hath all too short a date.
Sometime too hot the eye of heaven shines,
And often is his gold complexion dimmed;
And every fair from fair sometimes declines,
By chance, or nature's changing course, untrimmed.
But thy eternal summer shall not fade
Nor lose possession of that fair thou ow'st,
Nor shall Death brag thou wand'rest in his shade
When in eternal lines to time thou grow'st.
    So long as men can breathe or eyes can see,
        So long lives this, and this gives life to thee.

❤ WILLIAM SHAKESPEARE

Testimony

Love's Testament

O thou who at Love's hour ecstatically
Unto my heart dost evermore present,
Clothed with his fire, thy heart his testament;
Whom I have neared and felt thy breath to be
The inmost incense of his sanctuary;
Who without speech hast owned him, and, intent
Upon his will, thy life with mine hast blent,
And murmured, "I am thine, thou'rt one with me!"
O what from thee the grace, to me the prize,
And what to Love the glory,—when the whole
Of the deep stair thou tread'st to the dim shoal
And weary water of the place of sighs,
And there dost work deliverance, as thine eyes
Draw up my prisoned spirit to thy soul!

❤ DANTE GABRIEL ROSSETTI

If This Be Love,
To Draw a Weary Breath

*I*f this be love, to draw a weary breath,
To paint on floods till the shore cry to th'air;
With downward looks, still reading on the earth
The sad memorials of my love's despair:

If this be love, to war against my soul,
Lie down to wail, rise up to sigh and grieve,
The never-resting stone of care to roll,
Still to complain my griefs whilst none relieve:

If this be love, to clothe me with dark thoughts,
Haunting untrodden paths to wail apart;
My pleasures horror, music tragic notes,
Tears in mine eyes and sorrow at my heart.

If this be love, to live a living death,
Then I do love and draw this weary breath.

❤ SAMUEL DANIEL

Indeed This Very Love
Which Is My Boast

*I*ndeed this very love which is my boast,
And which, when rising up from breast to brow,
Doth crown me with a ruby large enow
To draw men's eyes and prove the inner cost,—
This love even, all my worth, to the uttermost,
I should not love withal, unless that thou
Hadst set me an example, shown me how,
When first thine earnest eyes with mine were crossed
And love called love. And thus, I cannot speak
Of love even, as a good thing of my own:
Thy soul hath snatched up mine all faint and weak,
And placed it by thee on a golden throne,—
And that I love (O soul, we must be meek!)
Is by thee only, whom I love alone.

❤ ELIZABETH BARRETT BROWNING

Were I As Base
As Is the Lowly Plain

Were I as base as is the lowly plain,
And you, my Love, as high as heaven above,
Yet should the thoughts of me, your humble swain,
Ascend to heaven in honor of my love.
Were I as high as heaven above the plain,
And you, my Love, as humble and as low
As are the deepest bottoms of the main,
Wheresoe'er you were, with you my love should go.
Were you the earth, dear Love, and I the skies,
My love should shine on you like to the sun,
And look upon you with ten thousand eyes
Till heaven waxed blind, and till the world were dun.
    Wheresoe'er I am, below, or else above you,
    Wheresoe'er you are, my heart shall truly love you.

❤ JOSHUA SYLVESTER

Some Glory in Their Birth, Some in Their Skill

Some glory in their birth, some in their skill,
Some in their wealth, some in their body's force,
Some in their garments, though new-fangled ill,
Some in their hawks and hounds, some in their horse;
And every humor hath his adjunct pleasure,
Wherein it finds a joy above the rest,
But these particulars are not my measure,
All these I better in one general best.
Thy love is better than high birth to me,
Richer than wealth, prouder than garments' cost,
Of more delight than hawks or horses be;
And having thee, of all men's pride I boast:
    Wretched in this alone, that thou mayst take
    All this away, and me most wretched make.

❤ WILLIAM SHAKESPEARE

How Do I Love Thee?
Let Me Count the Ways

How do I love thee? Let me count the ways.
I love thee to the depth and breadth and height
My soul can reach, when feeling out of sight
For the ends of Being and ideal Grace.
I love thee to the level of everyday's
Most quiet need, by sun and candle-light.
I love thee freely, as men strive for Right;
I love thee purely, as they turn from Praise.
I love thee with the passion put to use
In my old griefs, and with my childhood's faith.
I love thee with a love I seemed to lose
With my lost saints,—I love thee with the breath,
Smiles, tears, of all my life!—and, if God choose,
I shall but love thee better after death.

❤ ELIZABETH BARRETT BROWNING

My Mistress' Eyes Are Nothing Like the Sun

My mistress' eyes are nothing like the sun;
Coral is far more red than her lips' red;
If snow be white, why then her breasts are dun;
If hairs be wires, black wires grow on her head.
I have seen roses damask'd, red and white,
But no such roses see I in her cheeks,
And in some perfumes is there more delight
Than in the breath that from my mistress reeks.
I love to hear her speak, yet well I know
That music hath a far more pleasing sound;
I grant I never saw a goddess go,
My mistress when she walks treads on the ground.
    And yet, by heaven, I think my love as rare
    As any she belied with false compare.

❤ WILLIAM SHAKESPEARE

With the Same Heart, I Said, I'll Answer Thee

With the same heart, I said, I'll answer thee
As those, when thou shalt call me by my name—
Lo, the vain promise! is the same, the same,
Perplexed and ruffled by life's strategy?
When called before, I told how hastily
I dropped my flowers or brake off from a game,
To run and answer with the smile that came
At play last moment, and went on with me
Through my obedience. When I answer now,
I drop a grave thought, break from solitude;
Yet still my heart goes to thee—ponder how—
Not as to a single good, but all my good!
Lay thy hand on it, best one, and allow
That no child's foot could run fast as this blood.

❤ ELIZABETH BARRETT BROWNING

Faith

If Thou Must Love Me, Let It Be for Nought

If thou must love me, let it be for nought
Except for love's sake only. Do not say
"I love her for her smile—her look—her way
Of speaking gently,—for a trick of thought
That falls in well with mine, and certes brought
A sense of pleasant ease on such a day"—
For these things in themselves, Beloved, may
Be changed, or change for thee,—and love, so wrought,
May be unwrought so. Neither love me for
Thine own dear pity's wiping my cheeks dry,—
A creature might forget to weep, who bore
Thy comfort long, and lose thy love thereby!
But love me for love's sake, that evermore
Thou mayst love on, through love's eternity.

❤ ELIZABETH BARRETT BROWNING

The Forsaken

The peace which others seek they find;
The heaviest storms not longest last;
Heaven grants even to the guiltiest mind
An amnesty for what is past;
When will my sentence be reversed?
I only pray to know the worst;
And wish as if my heart would burst.

O weary struggle! silent years
Tell seemingly no doubtful tale;
And yet they leave it short, and fears
And hopes are strong and will prevail.
My calmest faith escapes not pain;
And, feeling that the hope is vain,
I think that he will come again.

❤ WILLIAM WORDSWORTH

To Mary Unwin

$\mathcal{M}$ary! I want a lyre with other strings,
Such aid from Heaven as some have feigned they drew,
An eloquence scarce given to mortals, new
And undebased by praise of meaner things;
That ere through age or woe I shed my wings,
I may record the worth with honor due,
In verse as musical as thou art true,
And that immortalizes whom it sings:
But thou hast little need. There is a Book
By seraphs writ with beams of heavenly light,
On which the eyes of God not rarely look,
A chronicle of actions just and bright—

    There all thy deeds, my faithful Mary, shine;
    And since thou own'st that praise, I spare thee mine.

❤ WILLIAM COWPER

If Thou Survive My Well-Contented Day

If thou survive my well-contented day,
When that churl Death my bones with dust shall cover,
And shalt by fortune once more re-survey
These poor rude lines of thy deceased lover,
Compare them with the bett'ring of the time,
And though they be outstripp'd by every pen,
Reserve them for my love, not for their rhyme,
Exceeded by the height of happier men.
O then voutsafe me but this loving thought:
"Had my friend's Muse grown with this growing age,
A dearer birth than this his love had brought
To march in ranks of better equipage;
    But since he died and poets better prove,
    Theirs for their style I'll read, his for his love."

❤ WILLIAM SHAKESPEARE

The Token

Send me some token, that my hope may live,
   Or that my easeless thoughts may sleep and rest;
Send me some honey to make sweet my hive,
   That in my passion I may hope the best.
I beg no riband wrought with thine own hands,
   To knit our loves in the fantastic strain
Of new-touched youth; nor ring to show the stands
   Of our affection, that as that's round and plain,
So should our loves meet in simplicity.
   No, nor the corals which thy wrist enfold,
Laced up together in congruity,
   To show our thoughts should rest in the same hold;
No, nor thy picture, though most gracious,
   And most desired, because best like the best;
Nor witty lines, which are most copious,
   Within the writings which thou hast addressed.

Send me nor this, nor that, to increase my store,
But swear thou think'st I love thee, and no more.

❤ JOHN DONNE

One Day I Wrote Her Name

One day I wrote her name upon the strand,
   but came the waves and washed it away;
   Again I wrote it with a second hand,
   but came the tide, and made my pains his prey.
Vain man, said she, that dost in vain assay
   a mortal thing so to immortalize,
   for I myself shall like to this decay,
   and eek my name be wiped out likewise.
Not so, (quoth I) let baser things devise
   to die in dust, but you shall live by fame:
   my verse your virtues rare shall eternize,
   and in the heavens write your glorious name.
Where whenas death shall all the world subdue,
   our love shall live, and later life renew.

❤ EDMUND SPENSER

To a Young Lady
Who Sent Me a Laurel Crown

*F*resh morning gusts have blown away all fear
 From my glad bosom: now from gloominess
 I mount forever—not an atom less
Than the proud laurel shall content my bier.
No! by the eternal stars! or why sit here
 In the Sun's eye, and 'gainst my temples press
 Apollo's very leaves, woven to bless
By thy white fingers and thy spirit clear.
Lo! who dares say, "Do this"? Who dares call down
 My will from its high purpose? Who say, "Stand,"
Or "Go"? This very moment I would frown
 On abject Caesars — not the stoutest band
Of mailed heroes should tear off my crown:
 Yet would I kneel and kiss thy gentle hand!

❤ JOHN KEATS

Sonnet from Modern Love

By this he knew she wept with waking eyes:
That, at his hand's light quiver by her head,
The strange low sobs that shook their common bed,
Were called into her with a sharp surprise,
And strangled mute, like little gaping snakes,
Dreadfully venomous to him. She lay
Stone-still, and the long darkness flowed away
With muffled pulses. Then, as midnight makes
Her giant heart of Memory and Tears
Drink the pale drug of silence, and so beat
Sleep's heavy measure, they from head to feet
Were moveless, looking through their dead black years
By vain regret scrawled over the blank wall.
Like sculptured effigies they might be seen
Upon their marriage tomb, the sword between,
Each wishing for the sword that severs all.

♥ GEORGE MEREDITH

Remembrance

Remember

Remember me when I am gone away,
Gone far away into the silent land;
When you can no more hold me by the hand,
Nor I half turn to go, yet turning stay.
Remember me when no more, day by day,
You tell me of our future that you planned,
Only remember me; you understand
It will be late to counsel then or pray.
Yet if you should forget me for a while
And afterwards remember, do not grieve;
For if the darkness and corruption leave
A vestige of the thoughts that once I had,
Better by far you should forget and smile
Than that you should remember and be sad.

❤ CHRISTINA ROSSETTI

Weary With Toil, I Haste Me to my Bed

Weary with toil, I haste me to my bed,
The dear repose for limbs with travel tired,
But then begins a journey in my head
To work my mind, when body's work expired;
For then my thoughts (from far where I abide)
Intend a zealous pilgrimage to thee,
And keep my drooping eyelids open wide,
Looking on darkness which the blind do see;
Save that my soul's imaginary sight
Presents [thy] shadow to my sightless view,
Which like a jewel hung in ghastly night,
Makes black night beauteous, and her old face new.
    Lo thus by day my limbs, by night my mind,
    For thee, and for myself, no quiet find.

❤ WILLIAM SHAKESPEARE

TO—*

[A lady whom he saw for some few moments at Vauxhall.]*

Time's sea hath been five years at its slow ebb,
    Long hours have to and fro let creep the sand,
Since I was tangled in thy beauty's web,
    And snared by the ungloving of thy hand.
And yet I never look on midnight sky,
    But I behold thine eyes' well memoried light;
I cannot look upon the rose's dye,
    But to thy cheek my soul doth take its flight;
I cannot look on any budding flower,
    But my fond ear, in fancy at thy lips,
And hearkening for a love-sound, doth devour
    Its sweets in the wrong sense:—Thou dost eclipse
Every delight with sweet remembering,
And grief unto my darling joys dost bring.

❤ JOHN KEATS

Go, Valentine

Go, Valentine, and tell that lovely maid
 Whom fancy still will portray to my sight,
How here I linger in this sullen shade,
This dreary gloom of dull monastic night;
Say, that from every joy of life remote
At evening's closing hour I quit the throng,
Listening in solitude the ring-dove's note,
Who pours like me her solitary song;
Say, that her absence calls the sorrowing sigh;
Say, that of all her charms I love to speak,
In fancy feel the magic of her eye,
In fancy view the smile illume her cheek,
Court the lone hour when silence stills the grove,
And heave the sigh of memory and of love.

❤ ROBERT SOUTHEY

when In Disgrace with Fortune and Men's Eyes

When in disgrace with Fortune and men's eyes
I all alone beweep my outcast state,
And trouble deaf heaven with my bootless cries,
And look upon myself and curse my fate,
Wishing me like to one more rich in hope,
Featur'd like him, like him with friends possess'd,
Desiring this man's art, and that man's scope,
With what I most enjoy contented least;
Yet in these thoughts myself almost despising,
Haply I think on thee, and then my state
(Like to the lark at break of day arising
From sullen earth) sings hymns at heaven's gate,
    For thy sweet love rememb'red such wealth brings,
    That then I scorn to change my state with kings.

❤ WILLIAM SHAKESPEARE

I Think of Thee!

I think of thee!—my thoughts do twine and bud
About thee, as wild vines, about a tree,
Put out broad leaves, and soon there's nought to see
Except the straggling green which hides the wood.
Yet, O my palm-tree, be it understood
I will not have my thoughts instead of thee
Who art dearer, better! Rather, instantly
Renew thy presence; as a strong tree should,
Rustle thy boughs and set thy trunk all bare,
And let these bands of greenery which insphere thee,
Drop heavily down,—burst, shattered everywhere!
Because, in this deep joy to see and hear thee
And breathe within thy shadow a new air,
I do not think of thee—I am too near thee.

❤ ELIZABETH BARRETT BROWNING

Among the Gods

Into the Middle Temple of My Heart

*I*nto the middle Temple of my heart
The wanton Cupid did himself admit,
And gave for pledge your eagle-sighted wit
That he would play no rude uncivil part;
Long time he cloaked his nature with his art,
And sad and grave and sober he did sit,
But at the last he gan to revel it,
To break good rules and orders to pervert;
Then love and his young pledge were both convented
Before sad reason, that old Bencher grave,
Who this sad sentence unto him presented;
By diligence, that sly and secret knave,
That love and wit, for ever should depart
Out of the middle Temple of my heart.

❤ SIR JOHN DAVIES

Soon as the Azure-Colored Gates

Soon as the azure-colored gates of th' east
  Were set wide open by the watchful morn,
I walked abroad, as having took no rest
  (For nights are tedious to a man forlorn);
And viewing well each pearl-bedewed flower,
  Then waxing dry by splendor of the sun,
All scarlet-hued I saw him 'gin to lour
  And blush, as though some heinous act were done.
At this amazed, I hied me home amain,
  Thinking that I his anger caused had.
And at his set, abroad I walked again;
  When lo, the moon looked wondrous pale and sad;
Anger the one, and envy moved the other,
To see my love more fair than Love's fair mother.

❤ RICHARD LYNCHE

To G[eorgiana] A[ugusta] W[ylie]

Nymph of the downward smile, and sidelong glance,
  In what diviner moments of the day
  Art thou most lovely?—When gone far astray
Into the labyrinths of sweet utterance?
Or when serenely wandering in a trance
  Of sober thought?—Or when starting away,
  With careless robe, to meet the morning ray,
Thou spar'st the flowers in thy mazy dance?
Haply 'tis when thy ruby lips part sweetly,
  And so remain, because thou listenest:
But thou to please wert nurtured so completely
  That I can never tell what mood is best.
I shall as soon pronounce which Grace more neatly
  Trips it before Apollo than the rest.

❤ JOHN KEATS

cards and Kisses

Cupid and my Campaspe play'd
At cards for kisses—Cupid paid:
He stakes his quiver, bow, and arrows,
His mother's doves, and team of sparrows;
Loses them too; then down he throws
The coral of his lips, the rose
Growing on's cheek (but none knows how);
With these, the crystal of his brow,
And then the dimple of his chin:
All these did my Campaspe win.
At last he set her both his eyes—
She won, and Cupid blind did rise.

  O Love! has she done this for thee?
  What shall, alas! become of me?

❤ JOHN LYLY

Love Asleep

I found Love sleeping in a place of shade,
  And as in some sweet dream the sweet lips smiled;
 Yea, seemed he as a lovely, sleeping child.
Soft kisses on his full, red lips I laid,
And with red roses did his tresses braid;
 Then pure, white lilies on his breast I piled,
 And fettered him with woodbine sweet and wild,
And fragrant armlets for his arms I made.

But while I, leaning, yearned across his breast,
 Upright he sprang, and from swift hand, alert,
 Sent forth a shaft that lodged within my heart.
Ah, had I never played with Love at rest,
  He had not wakened, had not cast his dart,
And I had lived who die now of this hurt.

❤ PHILIP BOURKE MARSTON

A Plain Youth, Lady, and a Simple Lover

A plain youth, Lady, and a simple lover,
Since of myself a last leave I must take,
To you devoutly of my heart I make
An humble gift, and doing this I proffer
A heart that is intrepid, slow to waver,
Gracious in thought, discreet, good, prompt, awake,
If the great earth should to her centre shake,
Armed in itself, and adamant all over;
Not more secure from envy, chance, desire,
And vulgar hopes and fears that vex the earth,
Than wedded to high valour, wit, and worth,
To the sweet Muses, and the sounding lyre:
Weak only will you find it in that part
Where Love incurably hath fixed his dart.

❤ WILLIAM WORDSWORTH

I Thought Once How Theocritus Had Sung

I thought once how Theocritus had sung
Of the sweet years, the dear and wished-for years,
Who each one in a gracious hand appears
To bear a gift for mortals, old or young:
And, as I mused it in his antique tongue,
I saw, in gradual vision through my tears,
The sweet, sad years, the melancholy years,
Those of my own life, who by turns had flung
A shadow across me. Straightway I was 'ware,
So weeping, how a mystic Shape did move
Behind me, and drew me backward by the hair;
And a voice said in mastery, while I strove,—
"Guess now who holds thee?"—"Death," I said. But, there,
The silver answer rang,—"Not Death, but Love."

❤ ELIZABETH BARRETT BROWNING

Loving in Truth, and Fain in Verse My Love to Show

Loving in truth, and fain in verse my love to show,
That she, dear she, might take some pleasure of my pain:
Pleasure might cause her read, reading might make her know,
Knowledge might pity win, and pity grace obtain,

I sought fit words to paint the blackest face of woe,
Studying inventions fine, her wits to entertain:
Oft turning others' leaves to see if thence would flow
Some fresh and fruitful showers upon my sun-burn'd brain.

But words came halting forth, wanting Invention's stay,
Invention, Nature's child, fled step-dame Study's blows,
And others' feet still seem'd but strangers in my way.
Thus great with child to speak, and helpless in my throes,

Biting my trewand pen, beating myself for spite,
Fool, said my Muse to me, look in thy heart and write.

❤ SIR PHILIP SIDNEY

A Dance of Nymphs

Scarcely, I think; yet it indeed *may* be
    The meaning reached him, when this music rang
    Sharp through his brain, a distinct rapid pang,
And he beheld these rocks and that ridg'd sea.
But I believe he just leaned passively,
    And felt their hair carried across his face
    As each nymph passed him; nor gave ear to trace
How many feet; nor bent assuredly
His eyes from the blind fixedness of thought
    To see the dancers. It is bitter glad
        Even unto tears. Its meaning filleth it,
        A portion of most secret life: to wit:—
    Each human pulse shall keep the sense it had
With all, though the mind's labour run to nought.

❤ DANTE GABRIEL ROSSETTI

Love undone

Since There's No Help

Since there's no help, come let us kiss and part—
Nay, I have done, you get no more of me;
And I am glad, yea, glad with all my heart,
That thus so clearly I myself can free.
Shake hands for ever, cancel all our vows,
And when we meet at any time again,
Be it not seen in either of our brows
That we one jot of former love retain.
Now at the last gasp of Love's latest breath,
When his pulse failing, Passion speechless lies,
When Faith is kneeling by his bed of death,
And Innocence is closing up his eyes,
    —Now if thou wouldst, when all have given him over,
    From death to life thou might'st him yet recover.

❤ MICHAEL DRAYTON

A Witlesse Gallant

A witlesse Gallant a young Wench that woo'd,
(Yet his dull Spirit her not one jot could move)
Intreated me, as e'r I wish'd his good,
To write him but one Sonnet to his Love:
When I, as fast as e'r my Penne could trot,
Powr'd out what first from quicke Invention came,
Nor never stood one word thereof to blot,
Much like his Wit, that was to use the same:
But with my Verses he his Mistress wonne,
Who doted on the Dolt beyond all measure.
But see, for you to Heav'n for Phraze I runne,
And ransacke all APOLLO's golden Treasure;
    Yet by my Froth, this Foole his Love obtaines,
    And I lose you, for all my Wit and Paines.

❤ ANONYMOUS

Like as the Culver
on the Bared Bough

Like as the Culver on the bared bough,
   Sits mourning for the absence of her mate:
   And in her songs sends many a wishful vow,
   For his return that seems to linger late:
So I alone now left disconsolate,
   Mourn to myself the absence of my love:
   And wand'ring here and there all desolate,
   Seek with my plaints to match that mournful dove:
No joy of aught that under heaven doth hove,
   Can comfort me, but her own joyous sight:
Whose sweet aspect both God and man can move,
   In her unspotted pleausance to delight.
Dark is my day, whiles her fair light I miss,
   And dead my life that wants such lively bliss.

❤ EDMUND SPENSER

witchcraft by a picture

I fix mine eye on thine, and there
 Pity my picture burning in thine eye,
My picture drowned in a transparent tear,
 When I look lower I espy;
  Hadst thou the wicked skill
By pictures made and marred, to kill
How many ways mightst thou perform thy will?

But now I have drunk thy sweet salt tears,
 And though thou pour more I'll depart;
My picture vanished, vanish fears,
 That I can be endamaged by that art;
  Though thou retain of me
One picture more, yet that will be,
Being in thine own heart, from all malice free.

❤ JOHN DONNE

Farewell to Love

Farewell, sweet Love! yet blame you not my truth;
  More fondly ne'er did mother eye her child
Than I your form: *yours* were my hopes of youth,
  And as *you* shaped my thoughts I sighed or smiled.

While most were wooing wealth, or gaily swerving
  To pleasure's secret haunts, and some apart
Stood strong in pride, self-conscious of deserving,
  To you I gave my whole weak wishing heart.

And when I met the maid that realized
  Your fair creations, and had won her kindness,
Say, but for her if aught on earth I prized!
  Your dreams alone I dreamt, and caught your blindness.

O grief!—but farewell, Love! I will go play me
With thoughts that please me less, and less betray me.

❤ SAMUEL TAYLOR COLERIDGE

A Renouncing of Love

Farewell, Love, and all thy laws for ever;
Thy baited hooks shall tangle me no more;
Senec and Plato call me from thy lore,
To perfect wealth my wit for to endeavor.
In blind error when I did persever,
Thy sharp repulse, that pricketh ay so sore,
Hath taught me to set in trifles no store,
And scape forth, since liberty is lever.
Therefore, farewell: go trouble younger hearts,
And in me claim no more authority;
With idle youth go use thy property,
And thereon spend thy many brittle darts;
For hitherto though I have lost all my time,
Me lusteth no longer rotten boughs to climb.

❤ SIR THOMAS WYATT

The Hardnes of Her Harte
and Truth of Myne

The hardnes of her harte and truth of myne
When the all seeinge eyes of heaven did see,
They streight concluded that by powre devine
To other formes our hartes should turned be.
Then hers as hard as flynte, a Flynte became,
And myne as true as steele, to steele was turned,
And then betwene our hartes sprange forthe the flame
Of kindest love which unextinguish'd burned.
And longe the sacred lampe of mutuall love
Incessantlie did burne in glory brighte,
Untill my folly did her fury move
To recompence my service with despighte,
And to put out, with snuffers of her pride,
The lampe of love which els had never dyed.

❤ ANONYMOUS

The Day Is Gone, and All Its Sweets Are Gone!

The day is gone, and all its sweets are gone!
   Sweet voice, sweet lips, soft hand, and softer breast,
Warm breath, light whisper, tender semi-tone,
   Bright eyes, accomplished shape, and languorous waist!
Faded the flower and all its budded charms,
   Faded the sight of beauty from my eyes,
Faded the shape of beauty from my arms,
   Faded the voice, warmth, whiteness, paradise—
Vanished unseasonably at shut of eve,
   When the dusk holiday—or holinight—
Of fragrant-curtained love beings to weave
   The woof of darkness thick, for hid delight;
But, as I've read love's missal through today,
He'll let me sleep, seeing I fast and pray.

❤ JOHN KEATS

Youth Gone, and Beauty Gone

Youth gone, and beauty gone if ever there
　　Dwelt beauty in so poor a face as this;
　　Youth gone and beauty, what remains of bliss?
I will not bind fresh roses in my hair,
To shame a cheek at best but little fair,—
　　Leave youth his roses, who can bear a thorn,—
I will not seek for blossoms anywhere,
　　Except such common flowers as blow with corn.
Youth gone and beauty gone, what doth remain?
The longing of a heart pent up forlorn,
　　　　A silent heart whose silence loves and longs;
　　　　The silence of a heart which sang its songs
While youth and beauty made a summer morn,
Silence of love that cannot sing again.

❤ CHRISTINA ROSSETTI

His Remedie for Love

Since to obtaine thee nothing me will sted,
I have a Med'cine that shall cure my Love:
The powder of her Heart dry'd, when she is dead,
That Gold nor Honour ne'r had pow'r to move;
Mix'd with her Teares, that ne'r her true-Love crost,
Nor at Fifteene ne'r long'd to be a Bride;
Boyl'd with her Sighes, in giving up the Ghost,
That for her late deceas'd Husband dy'd:
Into the same then let a Woman breathe,
That being chid, did never word replie,
With one thrice-marry'd's Pray'rs, that did bequeath
A Legacie to stale Virginitie.
    If this Receit have not the pow'r to winne me,
    Little I'le say, but think the Devill's in me.

❤ MICHAEL DRAYTON

I Do Not Look for Love that Is a Dream

I do not look for love that is a dream—
    I only seek for courage to be still;
    To bear my grief with an unbending will,
And when I am a-weary not to seem.
Let the round world roll on; let the sun beam;
    Let the wind blow, and let the rivers fill
    The everlasting sea, and on the hill
The palms almost touch heaven, as children deem.
And, though young spring and summer pass away,
    And autumn and cold winter come again,
    And though my soul, being tired of its pain,
Pass from the ancient earth, and though my clay
    Return to dust, my tongue shall not complain;—
No man shall mock me after this my day.

❤ CHRISTINA ROSSETTI

Thou Hast Thy Calling to Some Palace-Floor

Thou hast thy calling to some palace-floor,
Most gracious singer of high poems! where
The dancers will break footing, from the care
Of watching up thy pregnant lips for more.
And dost thou lift this house's latch too poor
For hand of thine? and canst thou think and bear
To let thy music drop here unaware
In folds of golden fullness at my door?
Look up and see the casement broken in,
The bats and owlets builders in the roof!
My cricket chirps against thy mandolin.
Hush, call no echo up in further proof
Of desolation! there's a voice within
That weeps…as thou must sing…alone, aloof.

❤ ELIZABETH BARRETT BROWNING

Spiritual Love

Too Long I Followed Have My Fond Desire

Too long I followed have my fond desire,
And too long painted on the ocean streams;
Too long refreshment sought amidst the fire,
And hunted joys, which to my soul were blames.
Ah! when I had what most I did admire,
And seen of life's delights the last extremes,
I found all but a rose hedged with a briar,
A nought, a thought, a show of mocking dreams.
Henceforth on thee mine only good I'll think,
For only thou canst grant what I do crave;
Thy nail my pen shall be, thy blood mine ink,
Thy winding sheet my paper, study grave;
    And till that soul forth of this body fly,
    No hope I'll have but only thee.

❤ WILLIAM DRUMMOND OF HAWTHORNDEN

When Slow from Pensive Twilight's Latest Gleams

When slow from pensive twilight's latest gleams
'O'er the dark mountain top descends the ray'
That stains with crimson tinge the water grey
And still, I listen while the dells and streams
And vanished woods a lulling murmur make;
As Vesper first begins to twinkle bright
And on the dark hillside the cottage light,
With long reflection streams across the lake.
The lonely grey-duck darkling on his way
Quacks clamorous; deep the measured strokes rebound
Of unseen oar parting with hollow sound
While the slow curfew shuts the eye of day
Soothed by the stilly scene with many a sigh,
Heaves the full heart nor knows for whom, or why.

❤ WILLIAM WORDSWORTH

When I Have Fears that I May Cease to Be

When I have fears that I may cease to be
   Before my pen has gleaned my teeming brain,
Before high-piled books, in charactery,
   Hold like rich garners the full-ripened grain;
When I behold, upon the night's starred face,
   Huge cloudly symbols of a high romance,
And think that I may never live to trace
   Their shadows, with the magic hand of chance;
And when I feel, fair creature of an hour!
   That I shall never look upon thee more,
Never have relish in the faery power
   Of unreflecting love!—then on the shore
Of the wide world I stand alone, and think
Till love and fame to nothingness do sink.

❤ JOHN KEATS

On "The Story of Rimini"

Who loves to peer up at the morning sun,
  With half-shut eyes and comfortable cheek,
  Let him, with this sweet tale, full often seek
For meadows where the little rivers run;
Who loves to linger with that brightest one
  Of Heaven—Hesperus—let him lowly speak
  These numbers to the night, and starlight meek,
Or moon, if that her hunting be begun.
He who knows these delights, and too is prone
  To moralise upon a smile or tear,
Will find at once a region of his own,
  A bower for his spirit, and will steer
To alleys, where the fir-tree drops its cone,
  Where robins hop, and fallen leaves are sear.

❤ JOHN KEATS

Friendship

when to the Sessions of Sweet Silent Thought

When to the sessions of sweet silent thought,
I summon up remembrance of things past,
I sigh the lack of many a thing I sought,
And with old woes new wail my dear time's waste:
Then can I drown an eye (unus'd to flow)
For precious friends hid in death's dateless night,
And weep afresh love's long-since cancell'd woe,
And moan th' expense of many a vanish'd sight:
Then can I grieve at grievances foregone,
And heavily from woe to woe tell o'er
The sad account of fore-bemoaned moan,
Which I new pay as if not paid before.
 But if the while I think on thee (dear friend)
 All losses are restor'd, and sorrows end.

❤ WILLIAM SHAKESPEARE

In Tyme the Strong and Statelie Turrets Fall

*I*n tyme the strong and statelie turrets fall,
In tyme the Rose, and silver Lillies die,
In tyme the Monarchs captives are and thrall,
In tyme the sea, and rivers are made drie:
The hardest flint in tyme doth melt asunder,
Still-living fame in tyme doth fade away,
The mountaines proud, we see in tyme come under,
And earth for age, we see in tyme decay:
The sunne in tyme forgets for to retire
From out the east, where he was woont to rise:
The basest thoughtes, we see in time aspire,
And greedie minds in tyme do wealth dispise.

   Thus all (sweet faire) in tyme must have an end.
   Except thy beautie, vertues, and thy friend.

❤ Anonymous

To Mr. R. W.

Zealously my Muse doth salute all thee
Inquiring of that mystic trinity
Whereof thou and all to whom heavens do infuse
Like fire, are made; thy body, mind, and Muse.
Dost thou recover sickness, or prevent?
Or is thy mind travailed with discontent?
Or art thou parted from the world and me,
In a good scorn of the world's vanity?
Or is thy devout Muse retired to sing
Upon her tender elegiac string?
Our minds part not, join then thy Muse with mine
For mine is barren thus divorced from thine.

❤ JOHN DONNE

The Fairest, Brightest, Hues of Ether Fade

The fairest, brightest, hues of ether fade;
The sweetest notes must terminate and die;
O Friend! thy flute has breathed a harmony
Softly resounded through this rocky glade;
Such strains of rapture as the Genius played
In his still haunt on Bagdad's summit high;
He who stood visible to Mirza's eye,
Never before to human sight betrayed.
Lo, in the vale, the mists of evening spread!
The visionary Arches are not there,
Nor the green Islands, nor the shining Seas;
Yet sacred is to me this Mountain's head,
Whence I have risen, uplifted on the breeze
Of harmony, above all earthly care.

❤ WILLIAM WORDSWORTH

The End